House Visualization Technique

Heidi Eversole, MA, LPC, TF-CBT

ARCHWAY
PUBLISHING

Archway Publishing books may be ordered through booksellers or by contacting:

Archway Publishing
1663 Liberty Drive
Bloomington, IN 47403
www.archwaypublishing.com
844-669-3957

ISBN: 978-1-6657-3686-2 (sc)
ISBN: 978-1-6657-3685-5 (e)

Library of Congress Control Number: 2023900825

Print information available on the last page.

Archway Publishing rev. date: 01/16/2023

Dedicated to my husband, James, our two precious children, and my dear friends MJ, Marq and Ann. Thank you also to Patti Bresler, who encouraged me and gave of her own time to see this dream come true.

"Sometimes the people with the worst past, create the best future..."
Umar ibn Al-Khattab

Contents

The Author's Story

In June 2013 I returned from a deployment as an interpreter in Afghanistan. My story may sound familiar to those who have been there. During that deployment, the unit I worked with experienced a number of casualties, both wounded and killed. Then, in the last week of the deployment, a suicide bomber detonated himself in a market outside our base, and scores of locals were killed or injured. As a result, our base received most of the casualties, or at least the most critical injuries that the local clinic did not have the resources to handle. My role that night was to translate between those injured and those treating, and to comfort those who were dying. It was a difficult evening, full of tragedy and a few precious miracles.

My trip back to America was eventful, also. The trip required several flights, like hops from a smaller base to a bigger base to (finally) the main base, Bagram. On the last flight to get to Bagram, I boarded a midsize cargo plane along with about twelve other people and an up-armored Humvee. On the descent into Bagram, I'm not sure exactly what happened, but the Humvee began to shake and bounce around violently. A very brave aircrewman hung out the back of the open aircraft, hurriedly securing the vehicle. I put on my helmet as I watched the process, and, seeing the look on my face, so did the interpreter across from me. Thankfully we landed safely, I'm sure in no small part to that crewman. It wasn't until we landed that I learned there had been another plane crash at Bagram just a few weeks before, also involving aircraft carrying up-armored vehicles.

There are so many stories I would like to tell you about my experiences in Afghanistan. The amazing people I met. The new things I learned and the people to whom I said goodbye. It was stressful, though. Man, so stressful. When I returned, I was an emotional and mental wreck. I was having panic attacks, mental fatigue, numbness, hyper-vigilance, nightmares, and, probably worst of all, feeling disconnected from my friend and family as a result of my experiences. I knew even before I got on the plane back to America that I needed to find help as soon as I arrived home.

I didn't waste any time. I was calling local therapists in Portland from the airport the moment my plane landed. I must have called and left messages with six or seven therapists, with no particular knowledge of what I was looking for except someone to help me find relief. Only one called me back: MJ. I'm so thankful that she did. She has acted as a lifeline for me, and I will forever be in her debt.

For those who have begun therapy after a traumatic event, you know that healing from trauma is a difficult and visceral process. Healing from multiple traumas is even more so. For those who begin therapy and realize that their whole life has been littered with traumatic experiences and the weight of them suddenly becomes evident, you have my profound respect. For me, going through the process of therapy was nothing short of an upheaval of my entire life. I felt like I was rebuilding the foundation of my life—or at least repairing it significantly—all while attempting to grasp the emotional and mental health issues that had permeated my family for generations.

The theme of houses as part of a conscious therapeutic process actually came to me while I watched a movie (though I won't say which one. Hint: it has Leonardo Dicaprio in it). And I have dreamt of houses since I was a young child. In my dreams, it was always a different house, in a different place, but I was always searching through them. I would find hidden passageways or staircases or rooms. There were people and situations in different rooms that I needed to deal with or learn something from. It wasn't until I started my own therapy process that I began to use this analogy as part of a self-guided meditation. One day during my reflection time, I closed my eyes and asked, "If my mind were a house, what WOULD it look like?" At that instant, my house was created and I have been using House Visualization Technique (HVT) ever since. I could tell you more, and perhaps at some point I will, but not right now. I can assure you that it has been nothing short of transformational for me.

I have included a section on HVT stories from my clients and their experiences with this activity (names have been changed to protect privacy, and permission was obtained). If you feel like reading ahead to see what others have learned from their own houses, do so. Each story is a powerful example of the potential of this activity. However, this activity might not be for everyone. I urge you to listen to yourself if you begin to feel overwhelmed. I wish you the best of luck with only this advice: like any mental health activity, you will get out of it what you put into it. Only you know if you are being authentic here, but you are the only person who matters in this case. I'm confident that if your goal is to connect with yourself, you will absolutely be on the path toward healing.

Instructions

Instructions

1. Read through each lesson thoroughly and completely.

2. For the material to be effective, please spend *at least* fifteen minutes at a time in your "house." You can do multiple sessions for one lesson, but I encourage you not to do more than an hour a day in total. This exercise can be emotionally draining.

3. Either during or directly following each session, please take time to write down your discoveries. You can do this in one of two ways. You can answer the questions associated with the lesson as well as any additional information that seems important, noting these under additional information on the worksheet directly. Your second option is to keep a running journal as you tell the chronological story and discover new information about your house.

4. When recounting details about the house, do not worry if the symbolism of a particular detail does not immediately make itself known. Don't worry if there are things about your house that seem fuzzy/blocked/locked/dark/etc. This is a protective measure and will become clear at the appropriate time.

5. Please describe any details that you notice about the house, rooms, décor, etc. This includes how they appear to you, but also any noticeable smells, emotions, sounds, or memories that they evoke when writing. This exercise is about the meaning you take from these.

6. Remember, the material is already there; we are only giving form to it and seeing it in symbolic form as the subconscious reveals it. You are a witness to your own house, but it is the authentic self and the subconscious that are revealing it to you.

"Where ever you go, go with all your heart."
—Confucius

Step One: Psychoeducation

Step One-A: Connection

Step One-B: Visualization

Step One-C: Trauma

"Wherefore seeing we also are compassed about with so great a cloud of witnesses, let us lay aside every weight….and let us run with patience the race that is set before us,"
- Hebrews 12:1 KJV Bible

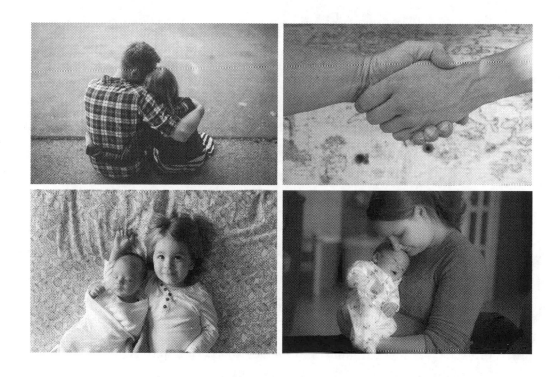

Step One-Part A: Psychoeducation on the Importance of Connection

There has been a tremendous amount of research into relationships and the importance of connection over recent decades. Specifically, the research on the importance of connection and its role in maintaining mental, emotional, and physical health. Connection between individuals has been studied directly and indirectly for centuries. But in the past two decades, one theme that has emerged in multiple studies is how detrimental loneliness is to an individual's health, mental, emotional and physical. In fact, some research has shown that loneliness might even shorten one's lifespan. One study in 2017 by Brown, Gallagher, and Creaven[1], discovered that loneliness negatively affected participants' ability to cope with stressors, particularly acute stress, which was found to cause elevated resting blood pressure and inflammation responses in the body of many of the participants.

At one point in our evolutionary history, our very survival was based on our ability to count on community. So much so, that isolation from community was and is still in some parts of

---

[1] Brown EG, Gallagher S, Creaven AM. Loneliness and acute stress reactivity: A systematic review of psychophysiological studies. Psychophysiology.

the world, considered a form of punishment in which the receiver would be without contact or limited contact with those on whom they emotionally depended. In times of COVID-19, I feel like most readers have perhaps a greater appreciation for what isolation means now than we might have only a few years ago. Prior to 2020, there were a few populations who might have been considered "isolated". Now, it is a term that is been sewn into our everyday vocabulary when talking about COVID-19. Not only that, but in becoming part of everyday life and survival, our community as a whole has faced a deeper understanding of how isolation impacts mental health both individually and collectively.

Isolation in the US prison system has been used for decades as a way to manage difficult or violent inmates. Though, even when a prison inmate receives solitary confinement, it is for limited amounts of time (or is supposed to be). That's because isolation from community and other people is so potentially devastating for an individual's well-being. Over the years, numerous studies on "isolation as punishment" have found that it's affects include psychosis, PTSD-like symptoms, suicidal thinking, and even cardiac issues in those subjected to it (please take note, US prison system). These findings have been echoed through the experiences of prison inmates, nursing home resident (especially in times of COVID-19), and, more recently, almost any population that has been required to self-isolate for a period of time due to COVID concerns. We absolutely need each other and need to connect. Being separated, even for a finite amount of time, even if key to survival, can be devastating to one's mental health.

I understand that using the examples of prison inmates and nursing home residents might be extreme examples. The example of those impacted by COVID-19, is not extreme, however. Living in isolation from each other has become the "new normal", though a kind of normal not many would ever wish for. If loneliness was a problem for some or many before, the quarantines that came with COVID-19 only exacerbated the feelings of isolation, hopelessness and loneliness. True, everyone experiences loneliness at some point. In 2020, Cigna released a report which had been a collaborative effort over the previous two years. It showed that, at that time, 61% of Americans reported feeling lonely regularly. In the same report, a further 40% reported that they felt their relationships "[were] not meaningful and that they [felt] isolated."[2] Imagine that: nearly half of the population feeling consistently and dishearteningly lonely. Imagine what those numbers would be if the report had been conducted after 2020.

Alas, while loneliness has become an increasingly present reminder of our disconnect from each other, there has been no decrease in the number of life events of which loneliness is a symptom. If anything, the number of losses has only increased. The loss of a loved one,

---

[2]   Novotny, A (2017). The Risks of Social Isolation. May 2019, Vol 50, No. 5.

whether it is a mother, father, grandparent, sister or brother. The loss of spouse or partner. The loss of a child (Heaven forbid). Loss can also include any current or past traumatic experience. Or attempting to process the onslaught of tragic events that happen all over the world we hear about daily. What's more, many mental health issues such as social anxiety, depression, acute stress, and post-traumatic stress, include physical and emotional isolation as a symptom accompanying them. It's important to understand the potential for a dangerous cycle between traumatic events or loss and co-occuring mental and emotional health issues. Without connection and support in the face of loss, loneliness and hopelessness can become overwhelming.

So, I know I've already talked about how important connection with others and how important relationships are. Connection with others acts not only as a protective factor for mental and emotional health, but also as a healing factor. One of the initial questions on most intake forms for mental health professionals specifically asks about an individual's social support system. In fact, one of the top predictors for successfully surviving and healing from a traumatic experience is a strong and stable support system. It's no secret that individuals thrive when surrounded by love and support. Unfortunately for some, that may not include family or maybe limited family members. Thankfully, it doesn't always have to be family, it can be anyone we bring into our lives who are loving and emotionally supportive. Having support and connection with others can help loneliness or isolation feel not so unbearable or daunting.

Okay, it seems like a good summary thus far would be: connection is the key to navigating our way through loneliness (and trauma healing and self-discovery, etc.). Yes. That can include connection with other people, our community, and even animals (I'm a dog person at heart). Actually, I'd like to add one more person to that list: yourself. I think that might be the most important one of all. Not only the most important, but the one from which connection with others grows. Connection with the authentic self is vitally necessary and out of this connection flows self-compassion, self-worth, hope, peace and resilience. It's also one of the connections most likely to be covered over with the mess of traumatic experiences, loss, or childhood abuse or neglect. Can you guess how much more difficult it is to connect with others if you are unable to connect with your authentic self?

So, this is my goal with HVT: to help individuals in the process of connecting or reconnecting with their own authentic selves. If that sounds both heavenly and scary, you're not alone. When someone says "Get out of your head" about this or that, it's as if being in your head or mind were a bad thing. All sorts of things exist out in the nebulous space of the mind. I think of the part in the movie *Insidious* where the father is searching for his son and must face the dark expanse of hell with just a lantern. I'm not trying to be dramatic. I think one's mind can feel like hell. It is entirely understandable that the expanse of one's mind would be scary for different reasons to different people, but specifically when we are talking about those burdened by whole range of mental and emotional wounds. Wounds which keep some in a small space afraid of confronting anything that might be lurking in the expanse.

I realize that might have been a little dark for some, so let me provide a more everyday example. Several years ago, as part of an advertising campaign, a number of landscape architects teamed up with school teachers to see if there were any psychological or behavioral changes in students when those students were presented first with a playground with no physical barrier surrounding it and then, later, the same play area surrounded by a fence. If it wasn't obvious, the goal of this study was to sell more fence installations. What they jointly observed was pretty amazing, though: when there was no physical boundary present around the play equipment, students stayed closer to their teacher and the center of the play area. However, after the fence was installed, children freely played in the entirety of the play area up to the boundary of the fence. Was there ever a more intriguing picture of safety within boundaries?

One huge difficulty with diagnoses like anxiety, depression, PTSD, acute stress, and bipolar disorder (just to name a few) is that the symptoms can feel nebulous, ghost-like, and without form like those things lurking in the expanse I mentioned. Of course, I'm not just talking about symptoms. I'm talking about memories up to and including pre-verbal. I'm talking about all the loss and abuse and traumatic experiences we've already decided are difficult to heal from. All of these things have little or no form to them, and as a result much of one's mind can feel menacing or intimidating, or even haunted. Can you see how it would be difficult to connect with one's authentic self if whole parts of an individual's mind were blocked off or avoided for emotional safety? Like many maladaptive traits, they are formed for survival and safety, not necessarily for healing.

Now, comes the bit about connecting (or reconnecting) with one's authentic self. This exercise is designed to help you provide—more accurately, it will invite your subconscious to show you—the boundaries of your own mind represented in the form of a house. By doing this, we "put the fence up" in the mind and allow our authentic self to speak into the house in a powerful way. Each individual's own subconscious provides form for those things which need to be seen and heard and healed. And does so in the context of safety and boundaries.

Maybe I should clarify—when I use the term "form", what I mean is a created internal idea of a thing that represents something else like symbols. In the context of HVT, symbols can include a locked door, a home with no walls, a picture on the wall, a piece of furniture, a trinket, an unopened box, the lightness/darkness of an area, or the color of an area. In the house of one dear client, she chose a dog, wound up and uncontrollable to represent her anxiety. Another client manifested a terrarium in the center of her house as a symbol of the growth and light she longed for. In my own house (more on that later), a mirror in the entryway of my home seemed to symbolize how true I was being to myself on any given day. In fact, I don't know that I would have enough space to share all the amazing, beautiful symbols I have heard come from the minds of my clients or personally experienced.

Lest this seem even just a little bit boring, hold on to your seat! I have a significant amount of anecdotal evidence which would contradict your assumption! I have found this simple exercise provides relief, hope, curiosity, self-knowledge, humility, inspiration and (not the least of which) healing for those who are brave enough to venture here. Even in those clients who were initially doubtful about the effectiveness of this exercise. Are you brave enough to venture in to find heal and restore your authentic self? By allowing your subconscious a blank canvas to give form and definition to your unique life and experiences, you become a witness to parts of the authentic self that have previously remained buried or avoided. Layer by layer, healing from deep wounds, happens though connection with the one person from whom you need validation and understanding: yourself.

One last note as I conclude step one: There may be parts of your house that you might not be able to see, that are locked or seem uncomfortable. Those are also boundaries and symbols. Honor them and be curious about them. It is a protective measure of your own mind. No need to force or pry your way into those places; they will be revealed to you when you are ready. Sometimes one's house can bring up intense emotions. Perhaps the important thing to know is that these emotions are *normal* and part of your story.

But I've gotten carried away. As with any journey, there are certain essentials that need packing. So, let's learn a little more about the information and tools that will be so very helpful as we prepare to cross the path to our house and dare to open the door.

Questions about Connection to Consider:

1. *What does connection mean to you?*

2. *Can you recall a time with you connected with someone strongly? What was that like?*

3. *How has connection with others (to include pets!) helped or hindered your mental health?*

> Lonely isn't being alone, it's the feeling that no one cares.
> —*Unknown*

Step One-Part B: Psychoeducation on the Benefits of Visualization

Maybe the best place to start is by answering the question "what is visualization?". According to Merriam-Webster, Visualization is defined as the "formation of mental visual images… the act or process of interpreting in visual terms or of putting into visible form."[3] In other words, it is the creation of an idea within one's mind which can then be shared verbally, in written form or artistically expressed. In terms of mental health treatment, visualization has usually been used as a technique to assist individuals and groups in coping with everything from everyday stressors to trauma processing. Interesting fact: visualization can also be used in place of an in vivo exposure when treating phobias or other avoidant behaviors. Visualization can be guided or free form and sometimes is used interchangeably with the term guided imagery. Because they are similar processes, I hope you will forgive me if I use them interchangeably also.

As you may already be aware, there is an inextricable link between the process of visualization and the imagination. The imagination plays a vital role in most individuals'

---

[3]   Merriam-Wester (2022). <u>Visualization Definition & Meaning - Merriam-Webster</u>

growth and development throughout the lifetime, but particularly in childhood. As we get older, imagination may become less of a part of our lives, more specifically, I think we begin trading the practical and tangible for the imagined. Perhaps that is what Peter Pan feared most: to grow up and forget the power of imagination. Alas, growing up is required, thankfully losing one's imagination is not. If you are one of those precious individuals who have kept your imagination alive and as part of your everyday life, good for you! If not, get ready to dust yours off! The amazing gift of imagination that was central to play and learning and relationships during childhood, is the very tool that you will need for HVT. Is it at all surprising that such a tool which helped us learn and connect with our surroundings in childhood would also be a wonderful tool to connect with our authentic selves in adulthood? I don't think surprising at all.

Let's begin with a simple visualization exercise that is an "oldie, but a goodie". I call the activity of the "Cup of Worry", though honestly, I didn't come up with this. I think I found it on Psychologytools.com. But it has been hugely helpful with most of my clients older than four. The activity is simply a picture of an empty drinking glass on a sheet of paper, drawn or printed. As the individual looks at the glass, they can ask "what am I worried about?". As the situations or people or relationship come to mind, I usually instruct a client to make a list down the side of the paper outside of the glass. There's no rush, so this can go on for several minutes or until the individual feels like they have a good summation of their worries. Next, you get to decide how those worries fit into your glass by drawing them as layers in your "Cup of Worry"(and color them if you so desire). Some will be thin layers and some will be thick.

Almost every client I have worked with, regardless of age, time-after-time, would find that their current stressors and worries had completely filled their cup to the brim or over-flowed. Then, in a moment of clarity, the lightbulb would come on and the connection between anxiety symptoms and this picture of an over-flowing glass would seem so obvious. It was from each of these client's own minds and imaginations that they had made the connection within themselves which required them to ask the question and listen for the answer. And with the answers, a sense of empowerment that the situation was definable. Don't believe me? Try it. I've attached the activity on the Resources page. You'll thank me.

While this is just a simple example, this is one of the simplest, but most profound (in my opinion) benefits of using visualization as a therapeutic tool. If lack of clarity or definability are significant parts of anything that causes worry or anxiety, when visualization is used, the authentic self is invited to fill that space and create the definition and, as a result, a sense of greater control over the situation. A simple activity that encourages connection with the use of the imagination and the authentic self brings clarity, empowerment, and hope. How refreshing is that?! But, that's not all. On a small scale, this exercise provides a visual which helps untangle a piece of what is going on emotionally and mentally (think of a ball of yarn or an old knotted necklace). When it comes to HVT, the house is a tool to continuously work out any troubling situation, past present or future and gather all of the same benefits.

Okay, so I've shared some anecdotal examples of visualization and its benefits. Now, let's talk about some of the research on the benefits, because the research is pretty significant. Mostly positive, to be honest. For example, one group of researchers in 2019 found that participants who used a guided imagery exercises before and during an MRI, showed significantly less anxiety in the identified areas of the brain than those individuals in the control group (who used no visualization). In another research paper published in 2019, researchers concluded that guided imagery acted as an effective alternative for anxiety and pain control with postoperative patients. Pain control?! How awesome is that! In fact, in the last decade, guided visualization has been shown to be a powerful therapeutic technique to decrease symptoms associated with stress, anxiety and depression. Now, here's the kicker. Visualization has ALSO been studied and found effective at managing symptoms from a whole host of ailments including hyperemesis in pregnancy[4], Cancer[5], Kidney failure (hemodialysis)[6], Diabetes[7], Multiple Sclerosis[8], Sleep Problems[9], Substance Abuse recovery[10] and PTSD[11]. That's not even the full list. Seriously, look it up on Google (or your search engine of choice). Talk about a versatile technique!

---

[4] Nasiri, S., Akbari, H., Tagharrobi, L., & Tabatabaee, A. S. (2018). The effect of progressive muscle relaxation and guided imagery on stress, anxiety, and depression of pregnant women referred to health centers.

[5] De Paolis, G., Naccarato, A., Cibelli, F., D'Alete, A., Mastroianni, C., Surdo, L., Casale, G., Magnani, C. (2019). The effectiveness of progressive muscle relaxation and interactive guided imagery as a pain-reducing intervention in advanced cancer patients: A multicentre randomised controlled non-pharmacological trial

[6] Afshar, M., Mohsenzadeh, A., Gilasi, H., Sadeghi-Gandomani, H. (2018).
The effects of guided imagery on state and trait anxiety and sleep quality among patients receiving hemodialysis: A randomized controlled trial.

[7] Azizi, S., Babaei, M., Mousavi, A., (2018). Investigating guided imagery on depression in patients with Type 2 diabetes.

[8] Case LK, Jackson P, Kinkel R, Mills PJ. Guided Imagery Improves Mood, Fatigue, and Quality of Life in Individuals With Multiple Sclerosis: An Exploratory Efficacy Trial of Healing Light Guided Imagery.

[9] Nooner, A. K., Dwyer, K., DeShea, L., Yeo, T. P. (2016). Using Relaxation and Guided Imagery to Address Pain, Fatigue, and Sleep Disturbances: A Pilot Study.

[10] Moe, T. (2011). GROUP GUIDED IMAGERY AND MUSIC THERAPY FOR INPATIENTS WITH SUBSTANCE ABUSE DISORDER.

[11] Jain S, McMahon GF, Hasen P, Kozub MP, Porter V, King R, Guarneri EM. Healing Touch with Guided Imagery for PTSD in returning active duty military: a randomized controlled trial.

Undoubtedly, Visualization has many benefits to offer. I, however, do not want to be neglectful to mention, that with those benefits there are also some challenges that may come with the process. Firstly, it takes practice to find a still place, emotionally and spatially. While this may be more easily accomplished sitting in a therapist's office, quiet and safe, with a trustworthy guide, not everyone has access to quiet, calm, or even safe places to practice at home. Trying to find that same stillness or calmness at home can be more difficult (not even the bathroom. Am I right, moms?). Emotionally, is can also be difficult because it takes practice to sit quietly long enough to embrace it. That part takes time, but if time is hard to come by, that might also make this difficult. If you have experienced these challenges, I offer my sympathy. If it were within my power, every person would have the space and time to connect with themselves. I can only offer the old therapy adage borrowed from the flight attendant's safety briefing, "You will need to put your oxygen mask on first, before you attempt to put one on the person in the seat next to you." Can you fill other's buckets if yours is empty?

Visualization is by no-means a cure-all, but it is one of the most adaptable and effective therapeutic tools that has real-life benefits for the mind and body. Almost every research group or study that has explored if Visualization would be effective for treating "X-Y-Z". Guess what? It is. Let's take hold of those benefits. Best of luck on the visualization of your house and all that you find inside it.

Questions to Consider about Visualization:

- *Can you think of a time when you used Visualization, whether as part of an assignment, a work project or a wellness exercise? What was the experience like?*

- *Have you experienced or anticipate experiencing any barriers to practicing visualization?*

Step One-Part C: Psychoeducation on Trauma

In the previous chapter I talked about the benefits of visualization as part of treatment for mental and emotional health issues. Those benefits are all great examples of how a simple tool can allow for foundational work in the healing journey of those who accept the challenge. Please note that I used the word "simple", not "easy". To better understand the challenges, I think it's important that we learn a little about what trauma is, what it looks like and what we can do about it.

House Visualization Technique was born in the midst of my own healing journey through trauma. Trauma that I had experienced, some I had witnessed and some which I had inherited from my family before me. The pathway through healing is particularly close to my heart and I'm so incredibly thankful to those who have walked with me through it. While I would like to take some time to discuss information about trauma, this is by no means an exhaustive guide to trauma. Merely a scratching of the surface, if you will. To anyone reading this who has experienced trauma or currently experiences any of the symptoms described in this chapter, I encourage you to seek out a mental health professional if you are not already working with one.

Let's start with a working definition of trauma. In recent decades the definition of trauma has been evolving. The Diagnostic and Statistics Manual for Mental Health Disorders, 5th Edition or DSM-5, defines a traumatic experience in the criteria for PTSD as "actual or threatened death, serious injury or sexual violence."[12] However, even at the time this was published in 2013, there was some disagreement in the mental health community concerning the narrowness of this definition. In the years since this was published, it is becoming apparent that the nature of what passes for "traumatic" is not only more complex but foundationally based on the perception of the one who experienced the event. For the purposes of this workbook, I prefer the definition listed on the website for the Department of Health and Human Services, which says, "Trauma occurs when frightening events or situations overwhelm a child's or adult's ability to cope or deal with what has happened." [13] This definition is the most inclusive and does the most efficient job at capturing the essence of a traumatic experience and it's effects.

Types of Trauma

It would not be possible to list all of the events which could be or have been perceived as traumatic, but I want to make sure that I provide a well-rounded idea of what a traumatic event might include. I also want to give the appropriate attention both to commonly acknowledged traumatic events and not-so-well-acknowledged traumatic events and situations. That said, I want to repeat that the perception of an event as traumatic is deeply personal and unique to an individual and that should be honored. Please take a moment as you read this to consider if or how any of these have impacted you in the past or are currently impacting you.

Abusive Relationships

Abusive Relationships can include ANY form of relationship: romantic partner, friend, mom, dad, sister, brother, aunt, uncle, grandparents, boss, or colleague, just to name a few. To clarify what I mean by abuse, I mean any repeated behavior that causes another person to feel unsafe or unequal in the relationship. This can take the form of verbal abuse (name calling, insults, screaming), psychological/emotional abuse (gaslighting, manipulation, isolating, threats against safety), financial abuse (limiting access to financial resources), or physical

---

[12]   DSM 5 pg****, ROI:

[13]   Department of Health and Human Services. Head start: ECLKC. Defining Trauma. Obtained from Defining Trauma | ECLKC (hhs.gov)

abuse (any non-consensual physical aggression). Abusive relationships can be and often are traumatic. If you find yourself in an abusive relationship currently or have experienced one in the past, this type of trauma may apply to you.

Violence

It seems like violence in the world around us, particularly in the news, has been more and more frequent lately. Violence, whether it is with a weapon or without. Whether it is intentional or accidental. Whether it is against people, animals or property. Or whether it is done privately or publicly, it has the potential be devastating to an individual physically, emotionally, and in so many other ways.

Natural Disasters

Ask anyone who has experienced a hurricane, a tornado, an earthquake, a tsunami, a wildfire, or a flood about the feeling of helplessness, fear and anger these kinds of events can evoke. One research team lead by Mary Alice Mills, Donald Edmondson, and Crystal L. Park, PhD in the weeks after Hurricane Katrina, interviewed evacuees at emergency shelters and found that 62% of the evacuees met the criteria for Acute Stress Disorder[14]. Additionally, they predicted that between 40-50% of those who developed ASD would go on to develop PTSD within the following two years as a result of having experienced hurricane Katrina. Furthermore, the Global Natural Disaster Assessment Report for 2020 reported that there were 313 major natural disasters in the year of 2020 "in 123 different countries and regions" which resulted in the deaths more than 15,000 people and affected almost a million people.[15] Of course these number are good data to have, but they do not tell us the individual stories of the survivors and the emotional challenges each faced as a result.

Death

The unexpected loss of a loved one, or Sudden Bereavement, can lead to a complex and complicated grieving process. In 2014, a research article published in the American Journal of Psychiatry, found that "Unexpected death was the most common traumatic experience and most

---

[14]   Mills, Mary Alice et al. "Trauma and stress response among Hurricane Katrina evacuees." *American journal of public health* vol. 97 Suppl 1,Suppl 1 (2007): S116-23. doi:10.2105/AJPH.2006.086678

[15]   2020 Global Natural Disaster Assessment Report (2021). Obtained at 1 (reliefweb.int)

likely to be rated as the respondent's worst, regardless of other traumatic experiences."[16] The researcher goes on to report that there is a significant connection between sudden bereavement and substance abuse, generalized anxiety, depression, panic and PTSD later in life.

Social Injustice

Issues of social justice have been gaining more and more attention in recent years. Rightly so. Just in the past two years alone, national attention has become focused on disproportionate violence toward specific groups of people based on race, socio-economic status, culture, religious beliefs or gender. Clinical Psychologist Lori Catz, in Psychology Today, calls the experience of this Injustice Trauma.[17] She goes on to describe that Injustice trauma "can manifest when people are mistreated, judged, blamed, humiliated, or neglected, or feeling unfairly blocked from resources, opportunities, or career advancement." Ultimately, according to the author, this can lead to distrust in the safety of an individual's surroundings, changes to their own self-concept or self-esteem, and effecting their ability to relate and attach with others in relationship.

Warzones

If you read the story at the beginning of the book, you'll know this one is close to my heart. Not just because of my own experiences, but for the amazing people we met abroad who had lived in those conditions for their whole lives. Some of them, for generations. As the US withdrew suddenly from Afghanistan at the end of 2021, it was impossible to escape the horrific news coverage of Afghans attempting to flee for their own lives and to protect the ones they love. I can tell you that watching this was heart-wrenching for every service member and every Afghan-American that I know.

Combat-related traumatic experiences and PTSD affect more than US service members and veterans. It affects the families of service members who await the service member's safe return. It affects refugees and asylum-seekers who search for safer life for their families. It affects those who continue to suffer in the oppression. And it affects those who watch the oppression but are helpless to stop it.

---

[16] Keyes, K. M., Pratt, C., Galea, S., McLaughlin, K. A., Koenen, K. C., & Shear, M. K. (2014). The burden of loss: unexpected death of a loved one and psychiatric disorders across the life course in a national study. *The American journal of psychiatry*, *171*(8), 864–871. https://doi.org/10.1176/appi.ajp.2014.13081132

[17] Katz, L. S. (2020). Injustice Trauma: Individual and Collective Distress. *Psychology Today*. Obtained from Injustice Trauma: Individual and Collective Distress | Psychology Today

The VA estimates that between Vietnam and Operation Enduring Freedom (Iraq/ Afghanistan), to include Desert Storm, between 11-30% of veterans suffered and may continue to suffer from PTSD symptoms.[18] Additional research by the VA showed that the PTSD symptoms experiences by a Service member has harmful results for their family including increases in marital/relationship issues and domestic violence.[19] In regard those who fled warzones, at meta-analysis by Blackmore et.al. in 2020 found that refugees and asylum-seekers have "high and persistent" levels of PTSD and depression.[20] Lastly, for those who watch but are helpless, this is called vicarious trauma and while there are few statistics, perhaps many of the readers of this workbook will recall a time when they experienced this.

Big "T" and little "t" Trauma

In the words of Elyssa Barbash, licensed Psychologist and therapist, trauma can be divided into two categories: Big "T" Trauma and little "t" trauma. Big "T" trauma is usually a big event where an individual fears death or serious injury for themselves or someone they care about. This kind of trauma is most associated with diagnoses like PTSD and often includes events like sexual violence, serious vehicle accidents, combat or domestic violence against a child or partner, just to name a few. Little "t" trauma are generally considered non-life threatening but still impactful events like bullying/harassment, emotional or verbal abuse, which usually happen over a period of time. Response to these types of events are specific to the individual and research shows that resilience has a significant impact on whether an individual is able to recover from little "t" trauma. However, both can lead to the experience of feeling "traumatized".

I want to be clear that too much little "t" trauma may seem less impactful but, as is often the case, little "t" trauma in general tends to include a greater quantity or duration of those events. And, as is also often the case, those who experience little "t" trauma throughout their lives will also encounter big "T" trauma at some point. Some would argue that most big "T" trauma was already preceded by little "t" in those who manifest with PTSD symptoms. [21]

---

[18] Obtained from <u>How Common is PTSD in Veterans? - PTSD: National Center for PTSD (va.gov)</u>

[19] Obtained from <u>Effects of PTSD on Family - PTSD: National Center for PTSD (va.gov)</u>

[20] Blackmore,R., Boyle, J. A., Fazel, M., Ranasinha, S., Gray, K.M., Fitzgerald, G., Misso, M., Gibson-Helm, M., (2020). The prevalence of mental illness in refugees and asylum seekers: A systematic review and meta-analysis. Obtained at <u>https://doi.org/10.1371/journal.pmed.1003337</u>

[21] Barbash, E. (2017). Different Types of Trauma: Small "t" versus Big "T". Psychology Today. Posted March 13, 2017. Located at <u>Different Types of Trauma: Small 't' versus Large 'T' | Psychology Today</u>

Signs and Symptoms of Trauma

It's not my goal that you walk away feeling able to diagnose another person, but more that you are able to recognize the signs and symptoms enough to get help from a professional (or encourage a loved-one with signs to get help). So, please keep in mind that I'm going to speak more generally, and not as much clinically. There are several diagnoses that include experience of trauma, so that's where this can become a little complicated, but in general there are a combination of signs or symptoms that might indicate someone is experiencing a traumatic response to past or on-going situation. No single symptom listed below means that you have PTSD, as some of these symptoms are comorbid with other mental health diagnoses. However, any symptom, if distressing is enough to seek medical and mental health care.

There are a couple of categories of signs and symptoms that I will try to keep organized for ease of the reader and for clarity.

- Sleep Issues
  - Lack of quality of sleep
  - Nightmares/Recurring bad dreams
  - Difficulty falling or staying asleep

- Response/Relational Issues
  - Hypervigilance
  - Heightened stress response
  - Being easily startled
  - Irritable
  - Rapid speech
  - Difficulty concentrating
  - Withdrawal
  - Dissociation.

- Emotional Issues:
  - Increased anxiety/depression
  - Shame/Guilt (i.e. "Survivors guilt")
  - Denial
  - Hopelessness
  - Rapid mood shifts

o   Avoidance due to fear of being triggered

o   Fear of more loss or death

o   Feeling emotionally numb or distant from friends and family.

I cannot over-emphasize just how important it is that you seek out professional help if you experience some of these symptoms. As we have discussed traumatic experiences come in so many forms that each person may respond differently to any given event. Please take a few moments before moving to the next chapter to use this as a tool and identify if there are any of these symptoms that are personally distressing to you. If so, reach out to a trusted friend or family member and begin the process of searching for a mental health professional.

Questions about Trauma to Consider:

- Have you experienced a traumatic event in your life? Do you know someone else who has? Does it fall into any of the categories listed in this chapter?

- Do you think it was Big "T" or little "t" trauma?

- What, if any, of the aforementioned symptoms do you experience and how often?

- Is there anything you have found to help you or someone you love begin to recover from a traumatic event?

"Don't rush over Hallowed Ground."- *Byron Kehler*

Step Two: Identifying Emotions

For the purpose of this activity, I will use this simple definition for emotions: internal signals about how you are interpreting your environment or a particular situation. Without emotion, life would be pretty boring. With emotion, all our experiences and relationships are enriched and color infused into life! They serve not just to bring warmth and joy, but can also bring sadness, fear, anger, and everything in between. Like a paintbrush, emotions color the world around us. True to the analogy, just like the color spectrum, those colors (emotions) can be bright and vivid, dark and intense, or light and airy, or really, any combination within. So, let's discuss how to identify and name emotions.

Please read the questions below, and answer in your own journal or the pages following:

1. Set a timer for one minute on your phone or watch. How many emotions you can list in that time?

2. Emotions come in all shades, like colors. On pages 111-112 there are several charts of emotions that you may have experienced at some point. Take a look and write down the emotions that resonate with you currently.

3. Can you remember a recent time when your emotions were strong or even overwhelming? What emotions were they (either positive or negative)? On a scale of 0-10, can you identify how strong each emotion was? Feel free to use the charts!

4. Think of some memories that bring up strong emotions. For instance, what is the happiest memory that you have? Perhaps a sad one, too? If you feel comfortable, write about those memories here. (Please start slowly. Like warming up for a workout, we are in the stretching phase of our exercise).

Step Three: Establishing Effective Coping Skills

If emotions can be helpful in interpreting our environment and situations, then knowing what to do with overwhelming emotions is also incredibly helpful. Emotions can become overwhelming for all sorts of reasons. It might be from a situation in the past or present, happy or sad or from something that acts as a trigger. Knowing what to do when emotions become overwhelming is the next most important thing after identifying those emotions. Having difficulty regulating strong emotions can negatively impacted behavior and relationships, so it is even more important to learn how to manage them through efficient coping skills. Now it's time to talk a little about what your personal coping strategies are. No judgement. Not many people have entirely healthy coping mechanisms at their disposal or even the resources to identify what healthy coping looks like. So, let's start with what coping mechanisms are currently in place and how to start incorporating some healthier coping skills.

Here are some questions to consider and answer:

1. In the previous step, you shared a situation or memory which brought up strong emotions. When emotions became strong or even overwhelming, what helped you get back to a calmer state? Can you identify how you returned to equilibrium, even if the emotions lingered afterward?

2. Have you discovered any activity that helps to calm you or keep you calm in stressful situations? Maybe something you do every day to help decrease or prevent stress or anxiety overall?

3. Would you say yours are healthy or unhealthy?

4. Do you know the difference between a coping skill and a coping mechanism? (Feel free to look this one up!) Give your idea here:

5. On the next page is a list of coping skills and distractions that research has shown can be effective to processing stress and strong emotions. Which of these would you be willing to try over the next week? Pick at least three and include when, specifically, you would plan to use them.

    *Additional resources are listed on pages 109-110 for online activities/ideas for most of these coping skills.

6. Make a specific goal to practice two of these skills (more than distractions, please) this week, and write those goals here. Don't forget to make it specific and measurable.

Goal one:

Goal two:

Ideas for Coping Skills

- Journaling: one of the best!! Just get it out and on paper! Some great places to start are:
  o what you are thankful for
  o what you hope for the future
  o letters to loved ones
  o letters to self, at different stages of life
  o free writing
- Social support: reaching out to a trusted friend or family member
- Hobbies: what are your hobbies? No judgment here! It could be knitting, video games (in moderation), baking, bug collecting, gardening, drawing, board games, a musical instrument, or any of a thousand others.
- Coloring: not just for children.
- Exercise routines: going for a walk, a run, a bike ride, or anything that gets your heartrate up and producing those endorphins!
- Meditation: guided meditation on a real or imagined safe place can be very helpful.
- Music: listening to comforting music can help stabilize emotions also. See the resources page for great suggestions.
- Grounding exercises: bringing yourself back into solid reality through sight, sound, smell, touch, and taste.
- Distraction: in a pinch, sometimes distractions like TV, cleaning, eating, or social media can be helpful to escape overwhelming emotions. The problem with distractions is that they are more about avoiding strong negative emotions than coping with them.

"Do not waste time bothering whether you 'love' your neighbor; act as if you did. As soon as we do this we find one of the great secrets. When you are behaving as if you loved someone, you will presently come to love him."
—C.S. Lewis, *Mere Christianity*

Can you accept this challenge toward yourself?

Step Four: Visualizing Your Inner House

Here we have arrived at the work of uncovering your house! Bravo and well done! Until now, we have been on the path to your house. Taking a few moments to emotionally prepare each time you approach your house, even for the first time, is an important part of the process of this experience. Take a few moments to practice deep breathing, listen to a moving song, read a impactful poem or passage, pray, or meditate. Whatever you choose, the goal is to increase the internal stillness and prepare to enter your own inner sanctuary.

Remember: if at any point you become emotionally overwhelmed, take a break, and use one or more of your coping skills. Respect the emotions you are experiencing.

1. Close your eyes, and ask yourself, "If my life, mind and experience were characterized by a house, what would it look like?" Allow the image to unfold. There is no time limit here.

2. What does it look like? Does it look familiar to you? If so, from where?

3. Can you describe the following things about it:

   - Is it a particular style of house?
   - What color is it?
   - Does it have a porch?
   - What color is the door?
   - What is the landscape or setting surrounding it?
   - Has it been well maintained?
   - What is the weather like where it is?

4. Now, visualize walking up to the front door. Take your time to notice anything that seems important as you approach your house. Again, there is no time constraint here. See if you can notice the following about your house:

   - Are there steps to the front door or porch? If so, what condition are they in?
   - If your house has a porch, is there anything on it?
   - Does the door have a window?
   - Is the door locked or unlocked? If it is locked, do you have a key?

5. Open the door and step inside. Take a moment to take in the experience of entering your house. This is important work and deserves to be allowed to unfold.

- Are there any sounds as you open the door? How about smells?
- What in the first thing you notice as you step inside?
- Does the door remain open or close behind you?
- What condition is the inside of your house in?
- Take some time to describe the experience of walking from outside to inside the door of your house in as much detail as you can.

6. Next, begin to explore the general layout of the house. It does not have to be precise, this is more like a general idea. This is more like a mosey (does anyone use that word anymore?) than a sprint. Remaining in a spirit of curiosity, consider the following questions:

- How many levels or floors does the house have?
- How many bedrooms are there?
- Where is the kitchen?
- Is there a living area, den, office, or dining room?
- Are there colors that stand out to you? Are there smells or sounds in specific rooms?
- Which rooms feel most comfortable or inviting?
- Are there any rooms that feel uncomfortable?
- Are there any rooms that are locked?
- Thus far, which room do you feel most drawn to?

7. As you prepare to conclude your initial visit, what are your general impressions of your house? Any thoughts, emotions, or memories that came to you during this initial visit? Make note of any details that seem important to you. Feel free to use this space to include any details not listed above.

8. Lastly, what about your house resonates with you? Is there something you learned during the initial visit?

9. If you feel like you need to draw your house to get a better visualization, use the page following this to do so.

Great job so far! Time to rest and allow yourself to process this first discovery.

"The noblest pleasure is the joy of understanding…"
Leonardo da Vinci

Step Five: Exploring Your House

Please allow at least a day between steps four and five!

1. As with the Step Four, please allow time to emotionally and mentally prepare for this exercise. A few deep breathes, a moment of meditation or prayer, a grounding with the earth. Do whatever helps gain stillness.

2. As you approach your house for the second time, do you notice anything different about the outside of your house from the initial visit? Take a moment to consider the following:

   • Setting of the house (urban neighborhood, country setting, on the beach, near a forest, etc.)

   • Is the setting familiar to you?

- Any exterior structures near the house
- Animals—either wild or domestic
- Previously unnoticed features on, near or around your house
- Landscaping
- Weather conditions

3. As you open the front door, what is the first thing you notice this time? What is the emotion or mood like in your home during this visit? Has anything changed?

4. Now we are going to do a little more work about the layout of your house. What is to your right and left as you stand in the entryway? Take some time to create visual a layout of you home if you need to.

5. Are you noticing anything different or new from the previous visit? Are there other people or animals in your house? If so, who are they and what are they doing?

6. Pick a room that seems comfortable to you and spend some time visualizing details as you look around the room. This could include furniture, décor, artwork, other doors, light fixtures, floor coverings or lack thereof, etc. Can you describe it?

7. Is there any symbolic meaning about these details? If so, what does it mean to you? (Note: Again, don't worry if not everything is completely clear)

8. Observe which rooms are generally less comfortable or maybe even inaccessible. Which rooms are they, and where are they located?

9. If you had to guess, what is it about or in those rooms that is uncomfortable? What do they symbolize for you? Can you identify any emotions they bring up?

10. Which, if any, of the rooms so far bring up memories? If so, which rooms? Are those positive or negative memories? Write about those memories here, even if they are little slivers of memory.

11. In the final part of exploring for Step Five, we are going to do a check for the attic and basement of your house. Your house may not have both and that's okay. Hypothetically, where would these spaces be, and how can you get to them (stairs, ladders, etc.)? Do you have impressions of their existence and what is contained within them? Please describe them below:

12. As you get ready to leave, what is your overall impression of your house? What did you learn during this visit? Were there any special meanings revealed as you connect with your authentic self?

If you are reading this, you are a ROCKSTAR!! Making it through the second visit is a HUGE step!

"Knowing is not enough; we must apply. Willing is not enough; we must do…"
Johann Wolfgang von Goethe

Step Six: Interpreting Elements of Your House

If you have already been doing this, great! If not, let's start to analyze some things that you have observed in your house. But first….

1. At the risk of sounding like a broken record, take time to invite in the stillness. Breathing and allowing yourself to be silent.

2. On this visit, the approach to the house is not as important. Step Six begins to transition from the introduction to the "getting-to-know-you" phase of this exercise. If the first two visits were dates, a third date means you might just have some hope for

this relationship. In this relationship, your authentic self is only waiting to be asked. Begin this visit opening the door.

3. As you stand in the entryway, are there details or features that have meaning to you? Some examples might include functional or decorative furniture, the presence or absence of lighting, the temperature in rooms, any sounds (or the lack thereof) that are present.

4. Explore the meaning of these items. What do these elements mean to you or are they attached to memories?

5. Can you choose which rooms seem the most important to you currently? Can you tell what is so important about these rooms? Perhaps they symbolize relationships, stages in your life, dreams, disappointments, or even traumatic experiences? What comes to mind?

6. Is the layout of your house static or dynamic? In other words, does the layout stay constant or do any of the rooms shift in shape or size? Does the size or shape of any room seem inconsistent with the overall layout of the house?

7. Notice if there are any other people or animals in your home. What are they doing? Do they notice or speak to you? Do you feel like you need to speak to them? What can you learn by observing these people or animals? What do they represent to you?

8. Which room or area seems to draw you in? If you have time, place yourself in that area. Notice as many details as you can. What sticks out to you and what do you think it means?

9. What have you learned on this trip about yourself? Has anything been revealed to you? (You can use the back of this page, too.)

Step Seven: Spending Time with the Uncomfortable

This step may be difficult for some readers. In fact, if it's not a little uncomfortable, you'd probably be missing the point of Step Seven. The pictures I chose at the top of this page were meant to represent those abandoned, neglected, lonely areas which we usually tend to avoid. This is your house, though. Discomfort is a sign that you are out of your comfort zone. Read that again. Like stretching for a workout, the initial discomfort of resistant muscles, begin to release with practice. This is that practice and the initial discomfort is part of the process.

Note: Step Six can be repeated as many times as necessary. There is no rush here and I encourage you to repeat Step Six as many times as you need. If your house were a new friend, how many get-togethers or coffee dates or girls' nights would you need to feel comfortable talking about the uncomfortable things? Some people are ready to dive deep into those types of conversations. Some need time to open up. Where do you fall on the continuum between those two? I encourage you to listen to your body and stop if you begin to feel overwhelmed.

1. Make this visit intentionally and with purpose. This step will require you to make an effort to spend time in a room that is uncomfortable. It is recommended to make this a shorter visit (sometimes, it's a good idea to set a timer for 3-6 minutes). Which room do you visit? What comes to mind while you approach this room?

2. Where is the room in the layout of your house? What happens while you walk into the room? Describe the details of the room. Do these details mean anything to you?

3. When you enter this room, can you sit down? If so, what are you sitting on? What do you notice about how you are feeling, as you remain in this room for the next few mintues? (As a note: don't forget to take a break if it becomes overwhelming!)

4. Is there anything you feel you need to do while in this room? Examples can include inspecting closets, opening drawers, looking more closely at artwork and pictures or looking out windows. This step is about exploration, not changing elements just yet.

5. If it is too difficult to stay in this room, can you describe the thoughts and emotions? Describe the experience of leaving once you feel like the emotions are less intense.

6. Is there any other room in the house you feel you need to visit or spend time in during this visit? This is completely up to you! If so, please describe this experience.

7. What do you feel you learned during this visit? Have you discovered new or different areas you think you will explore in the future?

"You yourself as much as anybody in the entire universe deserve your love and affection..."
Gautama The Lord Buddha

Step Eight: Giving Back to Your House

This begins the process of beginning to give back to your house and each reader's experience will be unique to them. For some, it will take only a few visits to their home to complete these tasks, for others it may take many more visits to complete. Don't be afraid to come up with some ideas of your own!

1. Prepare for this visit: a few quiet moments. Allow and move past any objections. The resistance is normal.

2. Are there parts of your house that are neglected? What areas of your house need care? What do those areas mean to you?

3. How can you begin caring for your house? Maybe it will be to dust, pull back the curtains, let fresh air in, repair wallpaper, or to create a more comfortable area. Perhaps it is just to be present with your house for a while. What comes to mind?

4. What does it mean to you to give back to your house?

5. Can you foresee any other projects that will need to be addressed in future visits, either on the inside or outside? What might they be?

Step Nine: Just Being at Home with Yourself

Like Step Six, Step Nine is meant to be repeated as many times as you like. If you have made it to this point, there's a good chance you have seen the benefit of HVT. I'd also be willing to bet that you have learned a great deal about your authentic self and have grown in understanding of your own mind and experiences. You're doing great! Keep up the self-care. Keep up the healthy coping skills. Keep up the growing!

1. Take a moment to center yourself.

2. What brings you to your house today? Has something happened that caused you to reach in to your house? Is there anything you are hoping to find?

3. Go to wherever you feel drawn in your house. Sometimes you may know before your close your eyes. Sometimes it may require a bit of wandering. Listen to your gut.

4. What new things do you discover? Just allow it to unfold, witness it, and honor the meaning of it to your life.

5. You can visit your house as often as you like, of course. Can you write about some of your experiences during your first Step Nine visit? Did you learn anything about yourself?

6. Some pages have been included for writing about your other Step Nine experiences. If you already have a journal or notebook, good for you! If not, feel free to use the Journal Entry pages beginning on page 89.

"Be yourself; everyone else is already taken…"
Oscar Wilde

Step Ten: Going Beyond the House

This has to do with exploring the environment surrounding your house: around, above, and below. I encourage you to utilize this option as you feel drawn. For some, this step will come naturally and details will be clear. For some, this may take practice and patience. Either way, whatever is revealed will have a special meaning for you and is worth exploring.

1. Around: What is your house surrounded by? It might be in a neighborhood, standing alone in a field, perched on the side of a hill or nestled in the trees of a forest. There are any number of possibilities.

2. Does the setting change at all? How far does it extend? How far would you need to travel to get out of this setting (this last one is a bit of an advanced question, but see if anything comes to mind)?

3. Where do you see your house and what does this setting mean to you? What does it tell you about yourself? Can you connect with this meaning?

4. I think this is a great place to observe and acknowledge and observe the weather around your house. It can change each time you visit, just like the time of day or the season. Each hold a different meaning.

5. Above: Are there any other things present in the space above your house? This might include bird, trees, powerlines, streetlights, or aircraft among any number of other possibilities.

6. Below: this could mean a basement or even under the basement. If you have gotten this far and have not discovered a basement, I encourage you to revisit that aspect of your house. Under your house could include water sources (like wells or cisterns), naturally occurring phenomena (caves or underground rivers or even ruins) or even bunkers. What, if anything, do you find and what does it mean to you?

Peace comes from within. Do not seek it without...
Gautama Buddha

Final Steps of HVT

"As long as you live, keep learning how to live…"
Seneca

Step Eleven: Potential Challenges While Visiting Your House

I thought it was only fair to include a chapter on some potential challenges in my experience with HVT, both with my own house and in working with clients using HVT. There seem to be a few common challenges that have popped up repeatedly. Rest assured, challenges are not an ending point, but an opportunity to allow the muscle to continue to stretch. Sure, it's uncomfortable and maybe frustrating, but the benefits will be obvious once the workout is in motion. So, let's talk about what some of the challenges could look like.

Mind block

A mind block could come in several forms. Some clients have reported not being able to picture a house at all or that "nothing comes to mind". Another similar complaint is that the initial picture which comes to mind is of a wall or fence or gate that is impassable for some reason. Some clients report knowing that their house lies beyond the obstacle, but for the moment, they cannot reach or even see it. Initially, as I developed HVT I also encountered a wall beyond which I could not see. It took a little practice before it dissolved. And, because this is an intuitive technique, it's okay that something might not initially be obvious to you. Intuition is a skill that needs to be allowed room to flow. And it requires some time. Please don't be discouraged if it doesn't seem obvious at first.

No Front Door

Yes, this one happens also. One individual was able to visualize their house and everything around it but could not find the door to get in. In his experience, the most effective strategy seemed to be to take time to walk around the exterior of the home and just observe. Eventually, what he found, was a secluded door, covered over by vines long ago. Inside, he discovered a home rich with memory and meaning. It took some time but allowing the questions to flow and curiosity to lead was the most effective way to overcome this challenge. And, of course, time.

Only Parts of Your House are Visible

This is also part of the process for some people. I would say it is one of the more exciting challenges. Like reading or watching a mystery story and having a feeling about the ending, but not knowing. Perhaps predictably, I say "give it time". Discover what you can about the rooms of the home that are within your ability to see. It is likely that there is something within those parts that you are being directed toward before you need to know more.

A "Haunted" House

This can manifest as a feeling about the house as a whole or about a part of the house. I can't say for sure, but I have a strong guess this one has to do with trauma (both Big T and little t). That said, these ghosts are there for your protection….at least for now. And later, they may have something to share with you. Some of my favorite scary movies are the ones where I find out at the end that the ghosts were attempting to protect the residents or warn them of danger. I think HVT ghosts are like that. Only the danger they are warning about happened in the past. Ghosts are still scary, though and being afraid to confront them is normal. Can you guess what my advice is? Yep. Give it time. Give the ghosts their space. They have been guarding this area for a long time, and it will take time to build courage to invite them into authentic conversation.

Overwhelming Anxiety

Does your anxiety go "through the roof" (pun intended) when you visit your home, or a specific part of your home? You're not alone. This is one of the most common challenges about HVT. If this happens while you are visiting your house, take a break, use your coping skills, do some self-care and make a mental note of the details surrounding the increase in anxiety. Is there a trigger that you can identify? Either way, go slowly. Healing rarely happens quickly and the most incredible discoveries can happen in the smallest of details.

Neuro-Divergence

For my neuro-divergent readers, I hope you will look over the Alternatives routes to using HVT after Step 12. In an attempt to do HVT during a recent session, one of my brilliant clients who has Attention Deficit Hyperactivity Disorder (ADHD) was able to modify the activity to help her focus and still capture the benefits of HVT! It was remarkable to witness and her insight has helped a number of other clients who are neuro-divergent!

I readily acknowledge that this list is not even close to exhaustive. Each person's experience of HVT will be as unique as they are, so there may be challenges that I haven't heard of or thought of. The most important factor to consider about any barrier is the personal meaning to you. If you are willing to be patient and curious about what lays beyond the barrier, I have no doubt that what you witness will be deeply and irreversibly moving.

Questions to Consider:

1. Have you experienced any of these barriers? If so, how did they present to you?

2. Were/Are there any barriers you experienced that are NOT mentioned here?

3. How did you overcome any barriers? Are you still in the process of overcoming them?

"Put your ear down close to your soul and listen hard."
Unknown

Step Twelve: Saying Goodbye (Maybe)

I debated with myself about including the idea of saying goodbye to one's house. At least in the initial HVT workbook. Primarily, because for those who are the more competitive among us, it gives the illusion of a finish line. I can say categorically that this is not the case. There is no finish line to see here. If there is a "goodbye" to be said, it is to a current house and to make room for a house that is more authentic to who you are. I think that's a sign of growth, and while we may find ourselves using our houses less and less as we grow into our authentic selves, I'm not sure that the work surrounding an individual's internal house will ever be completed.

Second, I think the process of HVT is similar to the stages of grief. I believe HVT is a way to pass through deep grieving, which unsurprisingly is also part of trauma recovery. I like to also compare it to reading your favorite book, listening to your favorite album or visiting a favorite place, only, because it's a person we are talking about, it's infinitely more complex. Like that book or song or place, each time you revisit, something new may catch your attention like a new detail that you had not previously noticed. Or maybe you will just see your house with a different perspective than previous visits. Like a cut gemstone, this practice is naturally multi-faceted, because that's just how brilliant the human mind is! And how brilliant YOU are!

You may spend many years exploring your house and learning from it. This is what I hope for all readers and how it happened for me when I initially began visualizing my house years ago. In 2013, it never occurred to me that I would say goodbye to my house, nor in the immediate years following. But, on fall morning of 2020, I got an inescapable feeling (remember this is about intuition) that I was in a process of saying goodbye each time I visited my house. So, I sat in each room and thanked it for what it had taught me.

Then, one morning, before I even closed my eyes, I knew this was the final visit. I could not fully see the house, like when you are so tired you can't keep your eyes open. I rushed from room to room to say a last goodbye. And, finally, almost ushered out of the house as if being pushed backward. The house was flooding, though not violently. As if being reclaimed by some force. As I stood in the foyer looking at the water, I realized there was something else that would stay with this house: me. Or this version of me. I had to "go down with the ship" or my house, in this case. I watched that version of myself sit cross legged on the floor of the foyer in the rising water as I was ushered out the front door. Then my eyes closed on that house and I have not been back since.

This can be a powerful moment when or if it comes time to say goodbye. It will be a moment of grieving, humility and a new beginning. It can also be scary to feel like you are starting over. Trust me, that house that comes after will be even more perfect than what you visualized before. It will be more authentic to you and part of the continued journey of healing and self-knowledge.

~Chronicles of Narnia, Aslan says to Lucy, "Courage, dear heart.~

Alternative Strategies for HVT

There those among us who, for whatever reason, really struggle with some of the parts of HVT that require focus, attention or even visualization. I read recently that there is a percentage of the population that literally cannot visualize something in their mind. It's called Aphantasia and it does affect a small, but important, part of the population. There're also my neuro-divergent friends with diagnoses like ADHD, Autism, Dyslexia, etc. I'd guess, there is not a person reading this workbook who has not been impacted by one of these diagnoses either through personal experience or with a loved one. Folks with these diagnoses are so much more than a label and absolutely deserve any of the benefits that HVT can offer them. To all the people mentioned and all those I have not mentioned (forgive me), I hope this helps!

I wish I could take all the credit for this part of the workbook. To be honest, there were some pretty amazing clients who stumbled on to a few of these. Special thanks to those clients (you know who you are) for your amazing insight and willingness to share so that others may benefit! Here are some of the alternative strategies for using HVT that may be a work-around to help with focus and, as a result, help neuro-diverse individuals grow closer to their authentic selves.

Write A Story

I usually assign HVT exercises as in-between session homework for my clients. I had one young lady who had significant difficulty visualizing her house. She also happened to have ADHD since childhood. It so happened at the next session she was telling me about the challenges with her homework and she followed by saying, "But I am writing a novel…." She went on to tell me what she had begun writing months before about a girl in a cabin on the edge of a wood. It was poetic and beautiful. And it didn't take long into listening her read her novel to recognize that this was her house. So, we explored the house in that novel, which she had been able to write about in great detail. It was an honor to witness her discovery not only of a part of herself that had been attempting to make itself known, but her emotional connection with her authentic self.

All of that is to say, if you have trouble with focus or being completely still or even visualization, write a story. Write a story about a person and a house. Any person, any house. You pick how to get to the house or where you find it. This story belongs to you and if you can allow it to flow, it will be meaningful.

Video Games

Yes, you read that one right. Specifically, the video building game SIMS can be helpful in creating something close to an actual visual aid for HVT. Additionally, there may be places (houses, castles, etc.) represented in a favorite video game that may resonate with you. It's okay to use those places and explore the meaning for you, even while actively in the game. Something similar, though a 2-D version can be accomplished with Graphing paper in creating a floorplan or drawing. If having a visual aid would be helpful, please consider trying either or both of these suggestions.

Artistically Inclined

This one is for those precious souls who have talent of which I can only dream. Specifically, for those of my readers who can draw, paint or sculpt, I highly encourage you to incorporate those talents into your use of HVT. Art is a beautiful means of self-expression and I have seen many clients harness their own artistic talents to process profound trauma experiences. I have also witnessed clients share visions of important moments in their houses through artistic expression.

Collage Creation

Virtual or material, creating a collage can be a terrific visual aid! Many of the pictures included in this workbook I found on Drexel and UpSplash. There are so many inspired photographers and artists who share their artwork openly on these sites and more. Would it be helpful to create a collage of pictures that represent your house? Maybe you've already stumbled on to a particular picture that resonates with you in some way. I encourage you to find more. I'll put the caveat here to be respectful of legal rights of photographs.

Questions to Consider:

1. Were any of these recommendations helpful for you? If so, which ones?

2. Did you discover a different way to augment your HVT experience that was helpful to you?

3. What did you learn about yourself through your modified experience with HVT?

"The only people who think there's a time limit on grief have never lost a part of their heart. Take all the time you need."
Unknown

Journal Pages for Visits

Pages for Future Visits

Date_____

Place I visited:

What I saw/heard/learned:

"The Mind is not a vessel to be filled but a fire to be kindled."
Plutarch

Date_____

Place I visited:

What I saw/heard/learned

"Be the person you needed as a child"
Unknown

Date_____

Place I visited:

What I saw/heard/learned:

"Grief never ends. But it changes. It's a passage, not a place to stay. Grief is not a sign of weakness, nor a lack of faith. Grief is the price of love."
Unknown

Date_____

Place I visited:

What I saw/heard/learned:

"Kindness is the language which the deaf can hear and the blind can see"
Unknown

Stories of Other Houses

I included this part of the book to help give a little encouragement and hope as you complete this activity yourself, as well as some examples of what others have experienced. Many people have been impacted by this exercise and have come away with the most authentic and beautiful pictures created by their own subconscious. I hope these mean as much to you as they did to me when I heard them.

Mina's Story: My Basement

When I began HVT, the basement of my home wasn't immediately clear to me. Maybe about a week after I initially discovered my house, I recognized the wood door at the back left of the foyer of my house. It was unassuming and not locked, and I already suspected what was there. It was a basement, lit by a pull string lightbulb at the bottom of the staircase. My basement was stone walled, small, and dark. It was damp and cold, but not scary. On the far side against the wall was a crib. My crib. And a rocking chair next to it. It was during this visit to my home that I realized how much nurturing I still needed and desired from myself. I spent several trips to my house simply rocking, holding my infant self in that basement.

Years later, this is also the room where I found my mother, also as a baby, hidden in a compartment in the stone wall. The compartment had been hidden to me before, but now I saw her: helpless, unaware, and afraid. I was powerless to stop how her life would impact her, but I was not powerless to have compassion for her now, in my heart, for how her life would turn out and mine as a result.

Hope's Story: Confronting Past Trauma

I was initially surprised to find my mother, who had passed away several years ago, in the basement of my house, folding laundry contently but not looking up or addressing me. It was during the processing of her death that I decided I needed to speak with her. So, I talked with my therapist about it and planned a time and date to accomplish this.

It was actually on the day before I planned to complete this that I experienced my house "calling to me." So, I put down what I was doing. Now was as good a time as any, right? I found my mom in the same laundry room. This time I brought my childhood stuffed dog, named Ada, to use as a conversation starter. I asked her if she remembered Juneau; she smiled and embraced me, sensing my discomfort with what I was there to say. I told her how I much I missed her and loved her. Then I asked all the burning questions I had: about why she'd done the things she'd done in my childhood and if she knew how much she had hurt me. I told her about how hard it was for me to accept my anger at her. Responding to this admission, she pulled out and handed me a coupon. When I was a child, mom's homemade coupons were always welcome gifts; though not fancy, they generally allowed us "permission" to do something we weren't usually allowed. This coupon said: "Permission to be angry." Angry at her, at the situation, at anything I needed to be angry at. We hugged again, and I said goodbye. I would be back to talk with her again. And she would be waiting for me.

Roger's Story

There is a bedroom. It's one of the few from my childhood. White walls with royal blue trim, the bedspread of cartoon characters and cars. On the walls are the posters of a fledgling and confused adolescent. The shades clash and clamor, but this is my domain, so it matters not. I am playing with my Lego toys and listening to music. The music makes me feel like an edgy, angsty teenager that nobody understands. Bizarrely, I like this feeling. I want to appear mysterious and brooding and intriguing to others. Then, I realize that I am playing with Legos. A child's toy. A feeling of shame washes over me. My emotions begin to spiral, and I think of my grandfather, who had passed a few years ago. I start to cry. It is confusing, because frankly I didn't much care for him. He was always short with us, and I don't remember hating him or loving him.

My mom opens the door and asks if I want lunch. I turn to her and watch her face drop as my tears flow. She asks me why I'm crying, and I tell her that I miss Grandpa, but that's not the whole truth. The source of the tears is a mystery to me, but I do know that tears will always get my mother's attention. Often, she will come running to comfort me, hugging me and making me feel whole.

She takes my hand and leads me to another place in the house. We open a door, and it's a strange hallway. Fluorescent light soaks the grey walls, and the curtains are closed, concealing adult patients. We step into one of the curtained areas, and I am so afraid but trust my mom. The crying of babies begins softly and grows louder and louder so that it blocks out all other sounds. We approach one of the babies, and it's me. I recognize this sickly pink creature with stitches across my belly and tubes running through me. I look to my mom for strength and reassurance, but I see her face. She is sobbing, and she is so scared and worried for me … and for herself. Will I live? Will I be too burdensome to care for? She feels like it is her fault, and I want so badly to take away her pain but cannot. I want to protect her. I pull her hand to leave and go back, but she won't budge, and I slowly begin to understand that she must stay. I let go and walk out. I can't be here anymore.

Paul's Story

The attic of my house isn't difficult to find. As soon as I enter it, it feels cold, dark, damp, and frightening. There are corners that I don't want to go into, and the ceiling is low so I can't stand upright. It becomes physically and emotionally painful to spend any amount of time in here. There are old cardboard boxes with worn-out labels, and I think to myself that I should throw them out … put them on the curb, perhaps, but I don't. I know it would feel good to stand back and see an organized, clean attic. I'd only need to look in the boxes briefly to determine if they should be trashed. Hmmm. This evokes a physical response from me, and I feel overwhelmed with the idea. I can't do this now, I'm just too busy with everything else—or why should I bother?

I'm not allowed to ignore it for long. My counselor challenges me to plan a visit to my attic with any added items to make the visit more comfortable. I brought a coat and an electric heater to help with the cold and a flashlight for light. I find it dusty and dirty and begin by cleaning the walls and the stairs leading to it. Then I put up a nice coat of soft beige paint to make the stairway look bigger and more inviting. I hang up some nice wall sconces and then install switches at the bottom and the top of the stairs for lights.

Now it is time to begin looking through the boxes. I know there is a box up here somewhere with holiday lights in it, and they are in the first box I look into. Memories of Dad and Christmas decorations come back to me, and I push forward. He never let us help with the tree or teach me put up the outdoor decorations, and the memory is hurtful. My dad struggled with being vulnerable enough to need help and with his lack of patience to teach. The strands are all neatly wrapped and taped so they don't tangle, as Dad would have wanted it, and I decide to string up the lights along the rafters. In an instant the attic becomes almost cozy, no longer frightening.

No time to rest; I create a workstation and continue going through the contents of the boxes. I am eager to get started and apprehensive about what else I might find.

Peter's Story

When I first contemplated what my house would look like, I had a difficult time getting started. Initially, I envisioned a country road with a gate that was preventing me from coming too close. Or, perhaps I could see the house off in the distance, but it was difficult to get to and difficult to imagine a layout. There were gates, long roads, or other obstacles in my way. I had to push past these to finally make it to my house.

Once there, my first impression of the ground floor was a very open and well-lit atmosphere. It was very inviting and my friends and family were all there. I envisioned the kitchen area, where everyone tends to hang out during parties. In fact, it was similar to my real house during a family gathering. Different groups of people gathered around each other talking and laughing. After more contemplation, I realized that these are the people that are most important to me—my immediate and extended family and my close friends. Everyone is there, and everyone is happy. This is where I enjoy spending my time but, unfortunately, not where I usually spend my time.

I ventured upstairs, and the image changed from a house to something that resembles an office setting with many small, segregated cubicles—dozens of them. I'm up here alone and bouncing around from cubicle to cubicle, conducting my daily business and leisure activities. Each cubicle represents a daily activity such as reading emails, spending time at my job, working around the house, playing on my phone, watching videos or TV, etc. Again, it's hectic, cold, and lonely up there, not an inviting place, but it's unfortunately where I spend most of my time.

It took several attempts before I could venture into the basement, and I continued to struggle with the idea of spending time there. I knew that the basement represented my soul, my engine, my true inner-being—and I knew that I almost never went down there and hadn't been for many, many years. I eventually made my way down the dark, scary steps.

What I found was my mom or a younger version of her—perhaps the age she was when I was ten or twelve. Dad was there too, but he was definitely in the background, watching us and happy to remain there for now. Mom was closer to me and passively observing me with care and concern in her eyes, inviting me to come closer, but at my own pace. When I approached her, she led me through the dark basement from section to section. As we walked the area immediately surrounding us was lit as if a light followed us, while the other sections stayed in darkness. She guided me on a sentimental journey, recalling all my best childhood memories—before her and my father's divorce. I remembered what it was like then—to be truly happy. Truly, truly happy—without a care in the world.

I have not been back. I'm not sure what else she has to say or to show me. I'm not sure I want to know. Can I continue to live my life without knowing?

Jeff's Story

Over the course of the past few months, I've been going to therapy to work on my anxiety. Part of my anxiety state that has weighed heavily on me has had to do with my family planning journey with my wife. Over the course of the past six years, we've had our daughter through IVF, but we've also experienced three miscarriages. We've tried to do what we can to deal with our grief over these losses, even going so far as to name these angel babies, but it became clear to me through therapy that I hadn't properly grieved these losses.

I ended up going through the HVT guided meditation of building my internal house, which I then wrote out. One of the rooms in this house was devoted to this family planning journey and included echoes of those three babies, who presented themselves at what their current ages would be today. It took me some time to build the courage to go into this room, and it was extremely difficult to do. Nevertheless, I took a few hours, typed out what was in my head, and cried nearly the whole time.

I spoke to each of them, expressing my sorrow and going through what I would like to hear from them. This allowed me to experience unaddressed emotions of loss, say things that I had not been able to say to each one, and take actual time to go through a true grieving process and honor their short existences. As a result, I ended up in a much better emotional state and am now able to think about these losses without fear of increasing anxiety. The internal house kept my angel babies as part of me and kept them safe until I was ready to address them. I still miss them each and the life they would have had, but now I feel like I know, at least for now, that I can talk with them as long as I need to continue processing these losses.

Michael's Story

When I first entered my house, I could not envision the entire outside, as much of it was overgrown with vines and vegetation. Upon entering my house I found a warm, well-lit and inviting living space that smelled of good food and a nice fire. The living area was inviting, with vaulted ceiling and exquisite craftmanship. I called this area "the living rooms."

The remainder of the house, its size, number of rooms, etc. were all kept from me. I called this area "the dark rooms." The rooms have *no* sunlight, and they do *not* breathe—not that they are dead. The rooms *are not* dead. There is a darkness, a despair, a danger, and fear that keeps me from exploring those rooms. It is like they are filled with some danger that seems elusive and not entirely known to me.

These rooms are *not* locked—I am certain of that. But, each room contains a **sentry**, like a butler—someone who works for me but acts more like a guard. The first sentry resembles the authority and malevolent characteristics of the bartender in a certain Stephen King movie from the '70s—having knowledge of pertinent facts but unwilling to share them. Pretending to have my best interests in mind but behaving like he does not. When I inquire about the room he guards, his response is polite, but adamant, "You don't belong here, you need to leave." And it takes several trips back to my house before I am willing to disregard his warnings.

It's several months later, and after many visits to my house, the "dark rooms" are no longer dark. No longer un-dead. And the sentries no long along beside them to warn me. Now, the same room I was warned against entering is light and filling with old blueprints cabinets, each holding pictures and memories. I call this my "research room," and now the only other presence I feel in this room is a loving and patient presence. I call it "The Librarian." I think it is God.

Lucia's Story

When I first discovered my house and began to visit, I described my house as two-storied, open and warm, and I could describe each floor and room. But my therapist asked which room in the home seemed most uncomfortable to me. For reasons I did not understand, I said, "living room."

As I visited my house over the following weeks, I was able to work out the meaning and symbolism of my rooms. I concluded that the living room bore a striking resemblance to my relationship with my father: no bright colors, functional but not inviting, and a little chilly. This was such a difficult realization for me.

It was not until several months later, after a particularly helpful and warm conversation with my father, which I had greatly appreciated, I returned to my home to find the living room housed a new piece of furniture: a lamp. It was tucked in the corner and gave off a warm light, both in tone and in temperature. I knew this corner of the living room was safe and comforting, and I could sit here whenever I came to the living room. This was a welcome addition to a room and relationship I had begun to grieve.

Maria's Story

I was having a particularly bad week. It had been more than a month since the traumatic event, and the waves still washed over me periodically. For days I would be consumed by sadness, pain, hopelessness, and despair in one of these waves, and it was at this time I went to visit my house.

I wasn't sure what I would find there, but the house I had left was beautiful, secluded, and airy like an art gallery. This time when I visited, though, I found the entire house shrouded, inside and out, in black and red. Pain? Sadness? Anguish? Probably all of them. This visual had been confined to a single room last time I was here.

I stepped into the main entryway, afraid. What should I do? I raised my hand, as if commanding something to rise from the floor. As I did, all of the black and red unveiled the house and swirled together on the floor in front of me until it formed a large spider, black and red and surprisingly cute. It wanted the attention it deserved, but I had been neglectful to give it.

I patted it on the head, and it walked with me side by side.

Anastasia's Story

My house is a beach house. When I initially visualized it, the first thing I noticed was that it sits close to the surf on stilts, like some of the homes I have seen along the coast. The stairs to the house that I use on my first visit are on the side facing away from the water. That door opens into the kitchen, which is small and decorated in an old-fashioned, but not unattractive way. On my second visit to my house, I use the door facing the water this time. It opens into a long, narrow hallway. The wallpaper and artwork are not anything I would pick and the hallway is uncomfortably tight. There is a stairway leading up and I am able to explore the upstairs of my home which is open and breezy. I feel at more at home here standing next to a window opened toward the ocean.

Several months later, I find the door to my basement. Still not visible on approach to the house, but I feel it drawing me learn what it wants to show me. To dust off hurtful memories of the past and begin to heal from them. This is the most difficult part of my journey so far and I am scared what has been stored in the boxes and trash bags that are stacked in the basement.

Rick's Story

The house that first came to mind was the classic American dream home. A house with red doors and shutters and the classic white picket fence. The yard was immaculate and green, plenty of trees and lush vegetation about. I walked to the door and opened it but was immediately transported into the living room of my childhood home. The home was a museum of sorts, one that my dad had transformed into a shrine dedicated to his three sons and their adventures. The walls were covered in posters, pictures of us at varying times in our lives, model airplanes hung from the ceiling in different poses. The house was truly unique. But it was also the place where my dad committed suicide 3 years ago. Upon learning of this tragic event, my family descended upon the house and with the help of many friends transformed it into a house we could sell. The day we sold it and gave away the keys, my heart broke as I walked away from the home for the last time. I can still feel the pain as I drove away, my wife and kids trying to console me.

So there I was stepping back in time, standing in this old house, (the way it used to be) as I worked through this visualization technique. My dad was not there, but I could feel his presence. I cry now even as I type this. I still have work to do in this house. I still have to let go of the guilt I feel over my dad's death. I still have to forgive him for leaving this burden and pain with us. I know I will meet him in this house. I know because I am willing.

"All their lives in this world and all their adventures in Narnia had only been the cover and the title page: now at last they were beginning Chapter One of the Great Story which no one on earth has read: which goes on forever: in which every chapter is better than the one before."—*C.S. Lewis, The Last Battle*

Resources

Coping Skills Resources

- **Journaling Writing Prompts**:
  - https://psychcentral.com/blog/30-journaling-prompts-for-self-reflection-and-self-discovery/
  - https://daringtolivefully.com/journal-prompts
  - https://penzu.com/journal-prompts
  - https://thoughtcatalog.com/jeremy-goldberg/2018/02/here-are-the-50-best-journaling-prompts-you-will-ever-read-or-need/

- **Social Support**- Please list here *who* you can reach out to in case you need to. Can you think of at least three people who have been emotionally and mentally supportive?

_____

_____

_____

_____

_____

***If you cannot think of people who have been emotionally and mentally supportive, I would *highly* encourage you to seek out professional mental health help. Please visit this website for your state's hotlines for emotional support and crisis assistance:

  - https://www.4help.org/?gclid=CjwKCAjw74b7BRA_EiwAF8yHFBJtGQvSm khSoglUpSeyGKO9npliDAGBqohuRYciKPAqcTBBhgvknRoCrXYQAvD_BwE

- Printable Coloring Pages!
  - o https://www.crayola.com/featured/free-coloring-pages/
  - o http://www.supercoloring.com/coloring-pages/arts-culture/mandala
  - o https://www.favecrafts.com/Adult-Coloring-Pages/Adult-Coloring-Pages-PDF

- Guided Meditation Videos and Bilateral Music
  - o https://www.youtube.com/watch?v=SEfs5TJZ6Nk
  - o https://www.youtube.com/watch?v=inpok4MKVLM
  - o https://www.youtube.com/watch?v=QHkXvPq2pQE
  - o https://www.youtube.com/watch?v=_k2HMSIxK0k
  - o https://www.youtube.com/watch?v=8dQXcnkHs6o
  - o https://www.youtube.com/watch?v=nTvvbguM6Cc

- Grounding exercises
  - o https://www.youtube.com/watch?v=1ao4xdDK9iE
  - o https://www.youtube.com/watch?v=_VybpoYlQ88
  - o https://www.youtube.com/watch?v=KeGybW3zuxo

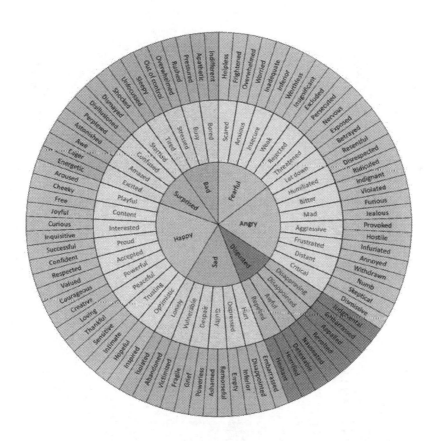

The Feelings Wheel

OPEN	LOVING	HAPPY	INTERESTED	ALIVE	POSITIVE	PEACEFUL	STRONG	RELAXED
free	devoted	blissful	fascinated	playful	inspired	calm	hardy	glowing
interested	passionate	joyous	intrigued	courageous	enthusiastic	content	secure	radiant
receptive	considerate	delighted	absorbed	energetic	bold	quiet	stable	beaming
accepting	affectionate	overjoyed	amazed	liberated	brave	certain	honest	reflective
kind	sensitive	gleeful	engrossed	exhilarated	daring	relaxed	reliable	smiling
harmonious	tender	elated	inquisitive	optimistic	hopeful	serene	sure	grounded
empathetic	attracted	jubilant	curious	frisky	exuberant	good	certain	unhurried
tolerant	admiring	euphoric	involved	animated	in the zone	at ease	dynamic	open-minded
understanding	warm	thankful	attentive	spirited	eager	comfortable	tenacious	efficient
easy	touched	festive	observant	thrilled	keen	pleased	composed	non-controlling
connected	close	ecstatic	amused	wonderful	earnest	encouraged	self-affirming	unassuming
sympathetic	loved	satisfied	thoughtful	funny	upbeat	surprised	truthful	trusting
friendly	sweet	glad	courteous	great	creative	bright	supportive	supported
approachable	gentle	cheerful	intent	giving	constructive	blessed	excellent	light
outgoing	compassionate	sunny	focused	sharing	helpful	assured	perseverant	spontaneous
flowing	caring	jovial		intelligent	resourceful	clear	responsible	aware
flexible	allowing	fun-loving		equal	motivated	balanced	energized	healthy
present	nonjudgmental	lighthearted		excited	cooperative	fine	sane	meditative
listening	appreciative	easygoing		enjoying	productive	okay	complete	still
welcoming	respectful	mellow		communicative	responsive	carefree	mature	rested
embracing	humble	happy-go-lucky		active	conscientious	adequate	solid	waiting
	gracious	glorious		spunky	approving	fulfilled	confident	laughing
	patient	innocent		youthful	honored	genuine		graceful
	honoring	child-like		vigorous	privileged	authentic		natural
	expansive	gratified		tickled	adaptable	beautiful		steady
	kindly	rapturous		engaged		forgiving		centered
	grateful	in good humor				sincere		placid
		in heaven				uplifted		
		on top of the world				unburdened		
						self-sufficient		

THE WORK OF BYRON KATIE

ANGRY		DEPRESSED		CONFUSED	HELPLESS	INDIFFERENT	AFRAID		HURT	SAD	JUDGMENTAL
enraged	mad	suicidal	pessimistic	lost	paralyzed	cold	terrified	insecure	tormented	anguished	stony
malicious	cross	directionless	dejected	disoriented	distraught	lifeless	petrified	wary	pained	desolate	hurtful
infuriated	retaliating	empty	glum	off-kilter	doomed	uncaring	panicked	menaced	tortured	devastated	brutal
violent	overbearing	desperate	cheerless	frenzied	distressed	uninterested	frozen	uptight	agonized	grieved	combative
vindictive	incensed	despairing	rotten	indecisive	pathetic	unresponsive	threatened	apprehensive	crushed	tearful	attacked
furious	upset	in hell	crabby	doubtful	overwhelmed	insensitive	hateful	guarded	deprived	sorrowful	tactless
repulsed	irritated	alienated	resistant	uncertain	shut down	numb	agoraphobic	defensive	rejected	unhappy	glaring
seething	controlling	miserable	punishing	distrustful	incompetent	reserved	fearful	troubled	humiliated	lonely	disgusted
scornful	agitated	masochistic	morose	misgiving	incapable	weary	suspicious	self-	insulted	mournful	ranting
hitting	antagonistic	despicable	cranky	unsure	alone	bored	rigid	absorbed	injured	dismayed	scolding
yelling	reprimanding	self-hating	grumpy	uneasy	fatigued	preoccupied	phobic	intolerant	offended	downhearted	obsessive
revengeful	envious	self-critical	burdened	tense	useless	robotic	disturbed	avoiding	afflicted	oversensitive	serious
hostile	reactive	self-	negative	stressed	inferior	slow	disrupted	unwelcoming	victimized	remorseful	stern
insulting	abrupt	deprecating	closed	argumentative	vulnerable	sluggish	anxious	unbending	heartbroken	sullen	frowning
swearing	quarrelsome	stuck	contracted	authoritative	inept	blasé	alarmed	paranoid	appalled	sour	recoiling
condemning	stubborn	ashamed	tight	condescending	incapacitated	blank	dreading	inhibited	wronged	self-	unfair
offensive	rebellious	exhausted	blocked	embarrassed	cut off		attacking	immobile	withdrawn	castigating	bossy
aggressive	exasperated	lousy	moody	hesitant	trapped		intimidated	attached	miffed	unworthy	stilted
bitter	impatient	tired	out of	shy	weak		nervous	prejudiced	indignant	fragile	stiff
loud	contrary	despondent	sorts	disillusioned	sick		scared	self-	suffering	disconnected	pushy
sarcastic	disrespectful	disheartened	no energy	uncomfortable	nauseated		worried	conscious	distant	blindsided	neglectful
frustrated	unpleasant	down	touchy	comparing	fidgety		frightened		invaded	discontented	stonewalling
resentful	annoyed	disappointed	haggard	dishonest	trembling		timid		bulldozed	crying	rude
critical	dictatorial	discouraged	drawn	demanding	craving		shaky		bullied	groaning	shrill
mean	sharp	powerless	slumped	distracted	squirming		restless		secretive	moaning	hard
sadistic	snapping	hopeless	slouching	blushing	jittery		cowardly		slighted	forlorn	fake
spiteful		grouchy	achy	awkward	woozy				smothered		phony
jealous		guilty	self-	conflicted	compulsive				belittled		shallow
short-		dissatisfied	loathing								territorial
tempered		sulky	crummy								complaining
		low	wretched								blunt
		bad									arrogant
		bummed out									superior
											faultfinding

Helpful Exercises for Visualization

The Worry Cup

In this exercise, create a list of things that are worried about and write them on the side or back on this paper. Then draw a line in the glass that indicates the "level" of worry you have for each.

Responsibility Pie

Think of a situation in which you feel tempted to assign blame to yourself or others. Next, create a list on the side of this paper for all the people that might have had some responsibility in that situation. Now, divide the pie (and color if you like) based on how much responsibility each person had. As you process and heal from this situation, observe if your Responsibility Pie changes.

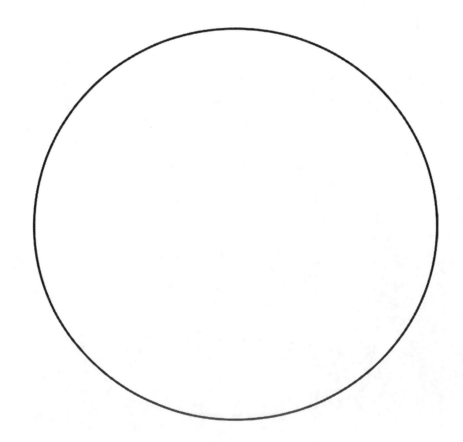

You're a Star!

I mean it! I love this one. Have you ever seen one of those beautiful Starburst Quilts at the County or State Fair? That's where I got this idea. I think life is like one or those beautiful colorful starbursts, in that each piece is beautiful on its own, some darker, some lighter. But each piece contributes to the pattern and each is always connected to the whole. Write in each diamond some part of your life: a memory, a relationship, a dream that is really important to you and then color!

You're a Gem!

This is very similar to the Starburst. Only this time, we're using the idea of a cut gemstone as an aid for visualization. The great thing about this one, is that it allows us to also use a 3-dimensional model for the visualization (like the iceberg analogy). The top view is similar to the Starburst, but the side view gives is an opportunity to view how the gemstone was shaped. I like to think of the point as our birth and the facets as those events which shaped you into the gem you are!

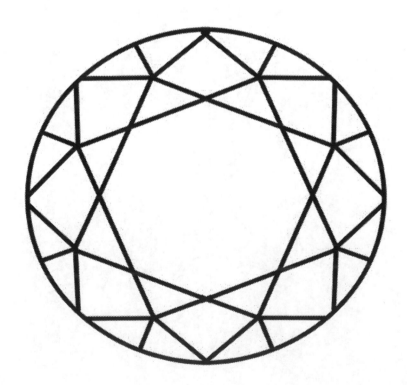

Name Your Dragon

This one might sound childish, but it really can be helpful. Is there some aspect of yourself that bothers you and that seems difficult to change? Chances are, you've got a dragon. It's okay, most people do at one point or another. As you color this page, think about what your dragon is. What would you name it? Where would you find it in your house?

References

References

Afshar, M., Mohsenzadeh, A., Gilasi, H., Sadeghi-Gandomani, H. (2018).

The effects of guided imagery on state and trait anxiety and sleep quality among patients receiving hemodialysis: A randomized controlled trial. Complementary Therapies in Medicine, Volume 40, 2018, Pages 37-41, ISSN 0965-2299. https://doi.org/10.1016/j.ctim.2018.07.006.

Andrus, C. (n.d.) Quote.

Azizi, S., Babaei, M., Mousavi, A., (2018). Investigating guided imagery on depression in patients with Type 2 diabetes. National Journal of Physiology, Pharmacy and Pharmacology. (njppp.com)

Barbash, E. (2017). Different Types of Trauma: Small "t" versus Big "T". Psychology Today. Posted March 13, 2017. Located at Different Types of Trauma: Small 't' versus Large 'T' | Psychology Today

Blackmore,R., Boyle, J. A., Fazel, M., Ranasinha, S., Gray, K.M., Fitzgerald, G., Misso, M., Gibson-Helm, M., (2020). The prevalence of mental illness in refugees and asylum seekers: A systematic review and meta-analysis. Obtained at https://doi.org/10.1371/journal.pmed.1003337

Brown EG, Gallagher S, Creaven AM. Loneliness and acute stress reactivity: A systematic review of psychophysiological studies. Psychophysiology, 2018 May;55(5):e13031. doi: 10.1111/psyp.13031. Epub 2017 Nov 20. PMID: 29152761.

Byron, K. (2016). Emotion list. The Work of Byron Katie. Obtainable at https://www.drkathrynkissell.com/resources/fantastic-list-of-emotions/

Case L.K., Jackson P., Kinkel R., Mills P.J.. Guided Imagery Improves Mood, Fatigue, and Quality of Life in Individuals With Multiple Sclerosis: An Exploratory Efficacy Trial of Healing Light Guided Imagery. Journal of Evidence-Based Integrative Medicine. January 2018. doi:10.1177/2515690X17748744

De Paolis, G., Naccarato, A., Cibelli, F., D'Alete, A., Mastroianni, C., Surdo, L., Casale, G., Magnani, C. (2019). The effectiveness of progressive muscle relaxation and interactive guided imagery as a pain-reducing intervention in advanced cancer patients: A multicentre randomised controlled non-pharmacological trial, Complementary Therapies in Clinical Practice, Volume 34, 2019, Pages 280-287, ISSN 1744-3881. https://doi.org/10.1016/j.ctcp.2018.12.014.

Department of Health and Human Services. Head start: ECLKC. Defining Trauma. Obtained from Defining Trauma | ECLKC (hhs.gov)

DSM-5 (2012). Definition of a traumatic event. Pg. 271.

Effects of PTSD on Family (2022). Obtained at: PTSD: National Center for PTSD (va.gov)

Feeling Wheel (n.d.) Obtained from http://feelingswheel.com/

2020 Global Natural Disaster Assessment Report (2021). Obtained at 1 (reliefweb.int)

Hampton, M. (2017). Fenced-in playgrounds: how boundaries can encourage greater creativity. Obtainable online at https://uxdesign.cc/fenced-in-playgrounds-d5f9371f8414

Henry, M. (2020). Nearly Two-Thirds of Adults in US Report Feeling Lonely. The Columbus Dispatch. Obtainable at https://www.dispatch.com/news/20200210/nearly-two-thirds-of-adults-in-us-report-feeling-lonely

How Common is PTSD in Veterans? (2022) – Obtained from: PTSD: National Center for PTSD (va.gov)

Jain S, McMahon GF, Hasen P, Kozub MP, Porter V, King R, Guarneri EM. Healing Touch with Guided Imagery for PTSD in returning active duty military: a randomized controlled trial. Mil Med. 2012 Sep;177(9):1015-21. doi: 10.7205/milmed-d-11-00290. PMID: 23025129.

Katz, L. S. (2020). Injustice Trauma: Individual and Collective Distress. Psychology Today. Obtained from Injustice Trauma: Individual and Collective Distress | Psychology Today

Kehler, B (2014). Personal Statement Quoted. Permission obtained July 2022.

Keyes, K. M., Pratt, C., Galea, S., McLaughlin, K. A., Koenen, K. C., & Shear, M. K. (2014). The burden of loss: unexpected death of a loved one and psychiatric disorders across the life course in a national study. The American journal of psychiatry, 171(8), 864–871. https://doi.org/10.1176/appi.ajp.2014.13081132

Lewis, C.S. *Mere Christianity* © copyright 1942, 1943, 1944, 1952 CS Lewis Pte Ltd. Used with Permission.

Lewis, C.S. *The Voyage of the Dawn Treader* © copyright CS Lewis Pte Ltd 1952. Used with permission.

Lewis, C.S. The Last Battle © copyright CS Lewis Pte Ltd 1956. Used with Permission.

Lewis, K. (2021). Guided Visualization: Dealing with Stress. National Institute of Mental Health. NIMH » Guided Visualization: Dealing with Stress (nih.gov)

Merriam-Wester (2022). Visualization Definition & Meaning - Merriam-Webster

Mills, Mary Alice et al. "Trauma and stress response among Hurricane Katrina evacuees." American journal of public health vol. 97 Suppl 1,Suppl 1 (2007): S116-23. doi:10.2105/AJPH.2006.086678

Moe, T. (2011). GROUP GUIDED IMAGERY AND MUSIC THERAPY FOR INPATIENTS WITH SUBSTANCE ABUSE DISORDER. Journal of the Association for Music & Imagery . 2011/2012, Vol. 13, p77-98. 22p. EBSCOhost | 82106671 | GROUP GUIDED IMAGERY AND MUSIC THERAPY FOR INPATIENTS WITH SUBSTANCE ABUSE DISORDER.

Nasiri, S., Akbari, H., Tagharrobi, L., & Tabatabaee, A. S. (2018). The effect of progressive muscle relaxation and guided imagery on stress, anxiety, and depression of pregnant women referred to health centers. Journal of education and health promotion, 7, 41. https://doi.org/10.4103/jehp.jehp_158_16

Nooner, A. K., Dwyer, K., DeShea, L., Yeo, T. P. (2016). Using Relaxation and Guided Imagery to Address Pain, Fatigue, and Sleep Disturbances: A Pilot Study.

Baider L, Uziely B, Kaplan De-Nour A. Progressive muscle relaxation and guided imagery in cancer patients. Gen Hosp Psychiatry 1994;16:340–7. Guided imagery | SpringerLink

Novotny, A (2017). The Risks of Social Isolation. May 2019, Vol. 50, No. 5. Obtainable at: https://www.apa.org/monitor/2019/05/ce-corner-isolation#:~:text=Hawkley%20points%20 to%20evidence%20linking,at%20every%20stage%20of%20life.

Renken, E. (2020). Most Americans Are Lonely, And Our Workplace Culture May Not Be Helping. Obtainable online at https://www.npr.org/sections/health-shots/2020/01/23/798676465/ most-americans-are-lonely-and-our-workplace-culture-may-not-be-helping

Thompson MB, Coppens NM. The effects of guided imagery on anxiety levels and movement of clients undergoing magnetic resonance imaging. Holistic Nursing Practice. 1994 Jan;8(2):59-69. DOI: 10.1097/00004650-199401000-00011. PMID: 8263086.

Many Thanks to the named and unnamed clients and colleagues
who lent pieces of their stories and expertise for this work!

Printed in the United States
by Baker & Taylor Publisher Services